EASY PIANO

STEELY DAN
GREATEST HITS

ISBN 978-1-4234-3208-1

HAL•LEONARD®
CORPORATION
7777 W. BLUEMOUND RD. P.O. BOX 13819 MILWAUKEE, WI 53213

Visit Hal Leonard Online at
www.halleonard.com

AJA

Words and Music by WALTER BECKER
and DONALD FAGEN

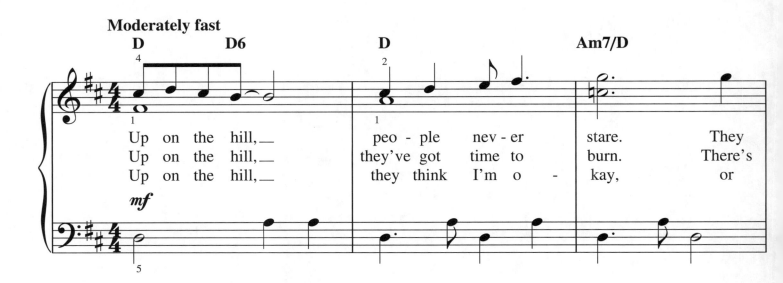

Moderately fast

D   **D6**   **D**   **Am7/D**

Up on the hill, —
Up on the hill, —
Up on the hill, —

peo - ple nev - er
they've got time to
they think I'm o -

stare.   They
burn.   There's
kay,   or

mf

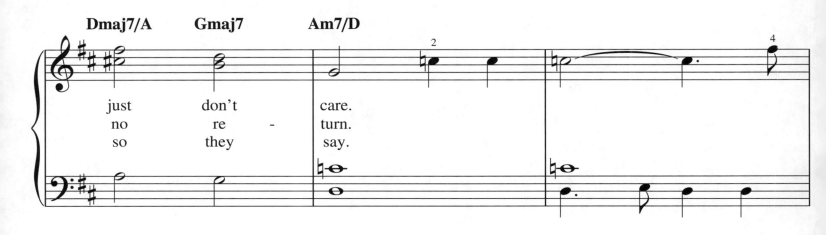

Dmaj7/A   **Gmaj7**   **Am7/D**

just   don't   care.
no   re -   turn.
so   they   say.

E♭maj7   **F6/9**

6

To Coda ⊕

BABYLON SISTERS

Words and Music by WALTER BECKER
and DONALD FAGEN

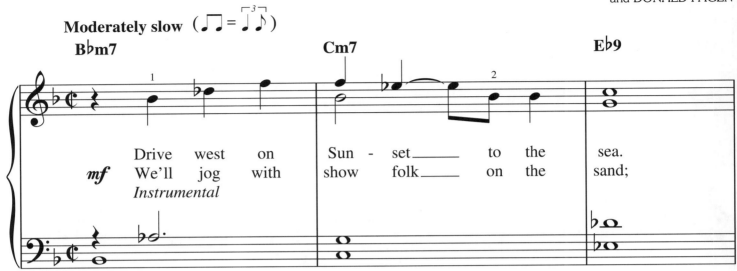

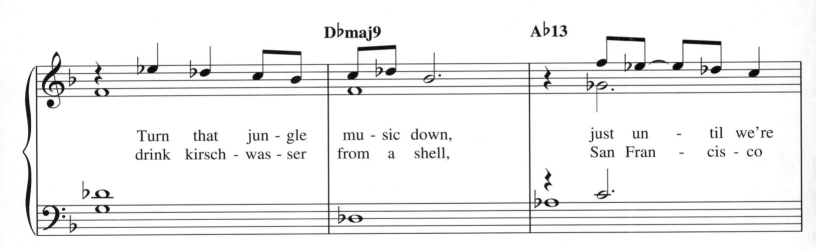

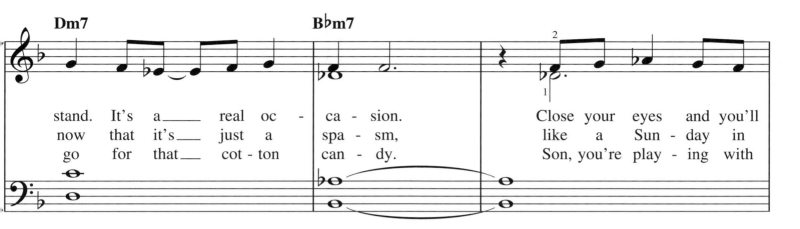

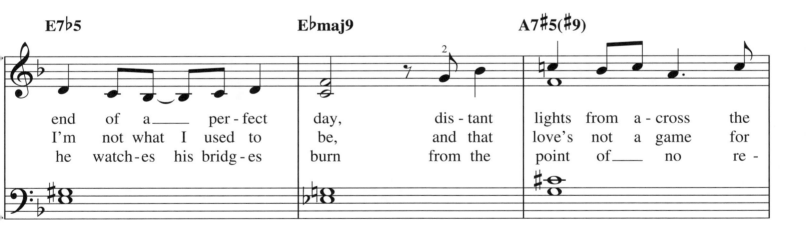

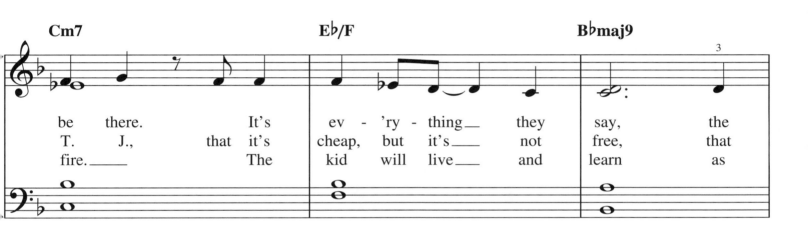

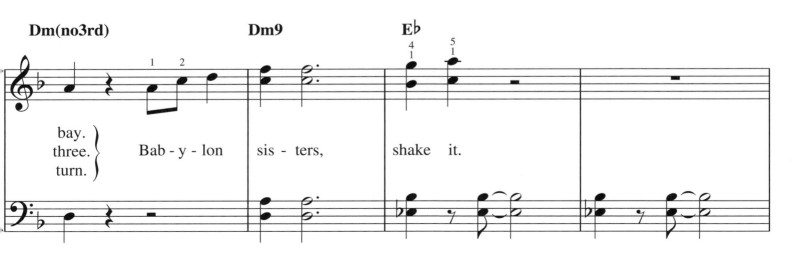

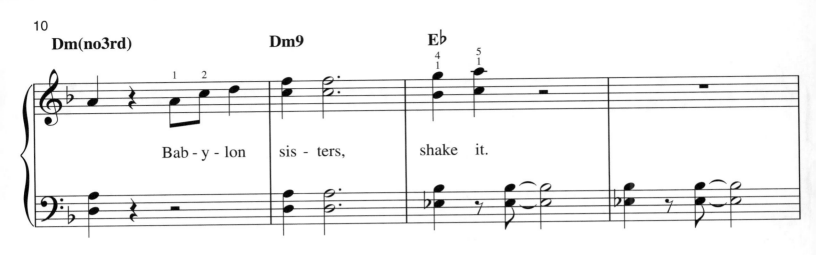

Dm(no3rd) · Dm9 · Eb

Bab - y - lon sis - ters, shake it.

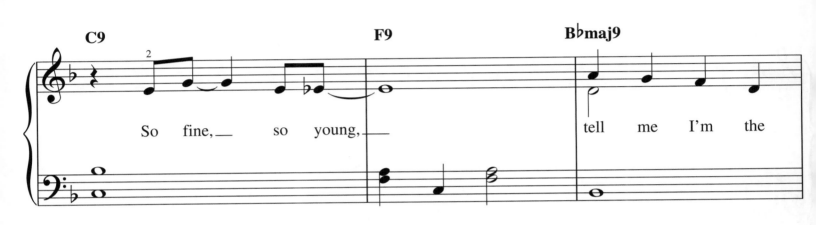

C9 · F9 · Bbmaj9

So fine,— so young,— tell me I'm the

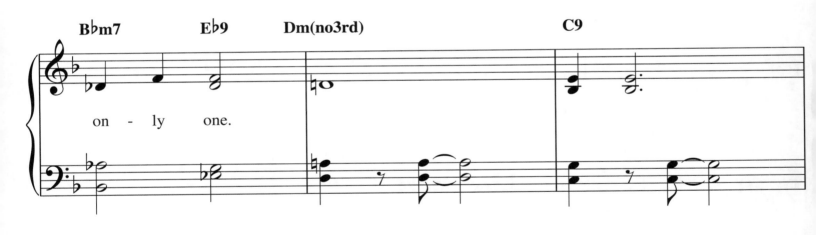

Bbm7 · Eb9 · Dm(no3rd) · C9

on - ly one.

To Coda ⊕

Eb · B/E · F#/E

D.C. al Coda

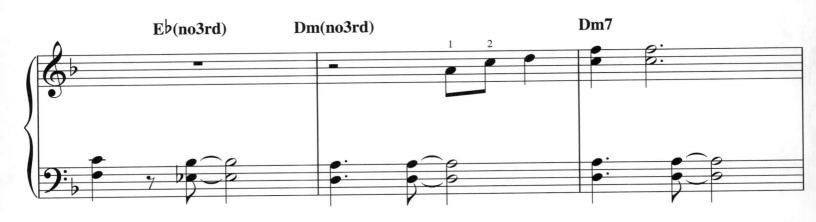

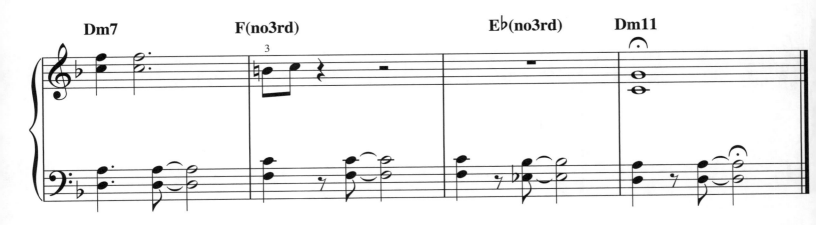

DEACON BLUES

Words and Music by WALTER BECKER
and DONALD FAGEN

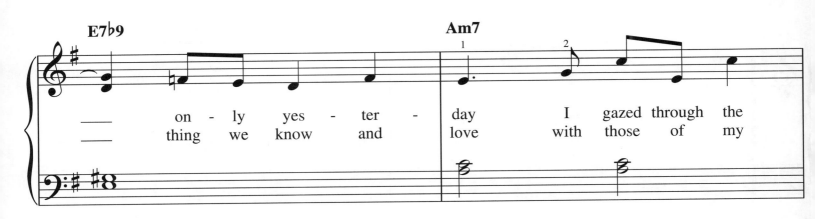

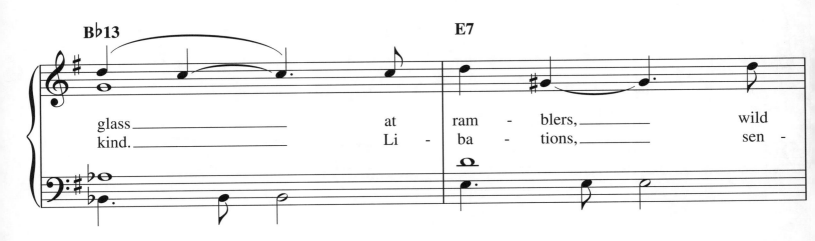

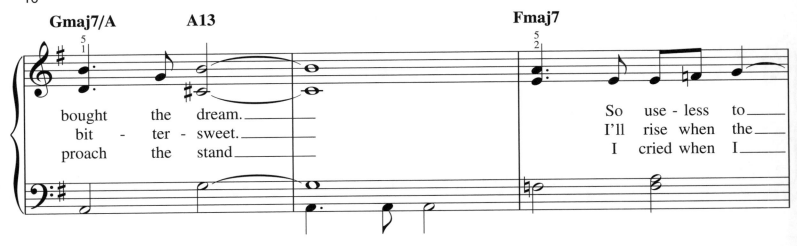

Gmaj7/A **A13** **Fmaj7**

bought the dream.
bit - ter - sweet.
proach the stand

So use - less to
I'll rise when the
I cried when I

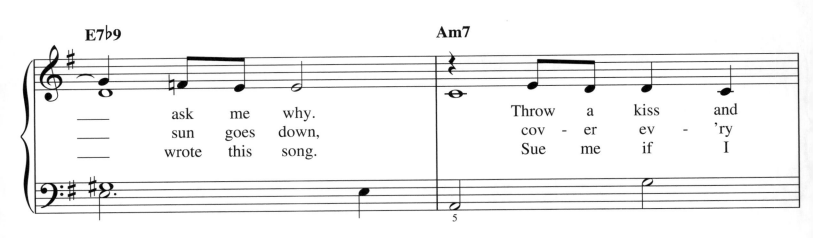

E7♭9 **Am7**

ask me why.
sun goes down,
wrote this song.

Throw a kiss and
cov - er ev - 'ry
Sue me if I

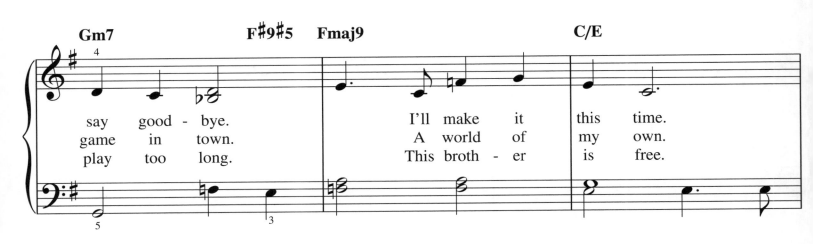

Gm7 **F♯9♯5** **Fmaj9** **C/E**

say good - bye.
game in town.
play too long.

I'll make it this time.
A world of my own.
This broth - er is free.

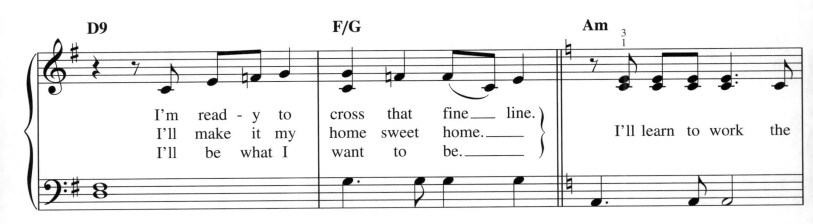

D9 **F/G** **Am**

I'm read - y to
I'll make it my
I'll be what I

cross that fine line.
home sweet home.
want to be.

I'll learn to work the

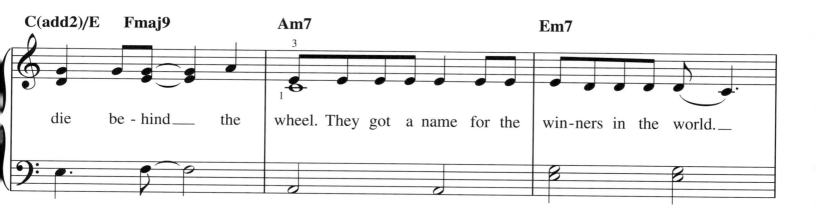

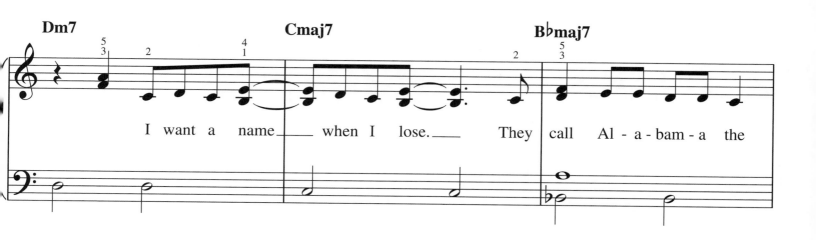

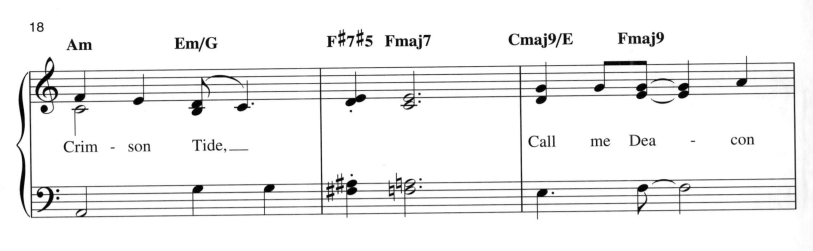

Crim - son Tide, ___

Call me Dea - con

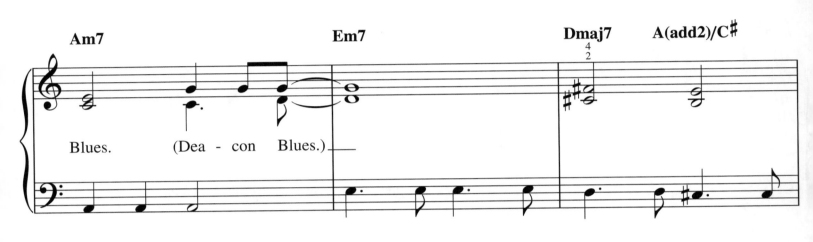

Blues. (Dea - con Blues.) ___

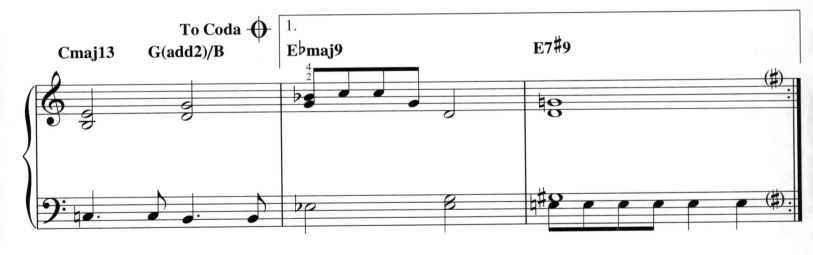

To Coda ⊕

1.

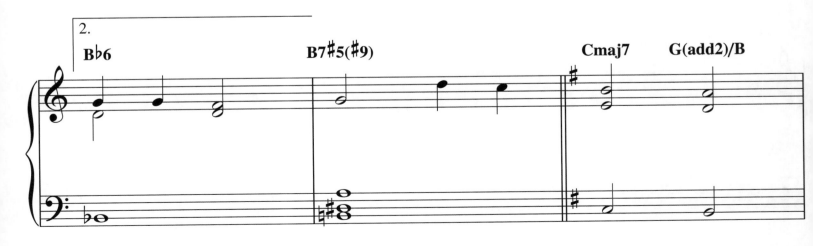

2.

DIRTY WORK

Words and Music by WALTER BECKER
and DONALD FAGEN

Times are
Light the

hard, you're a -
can - dle, put the

fraid to pay the
lock up - on the

fee, so you
door; you have

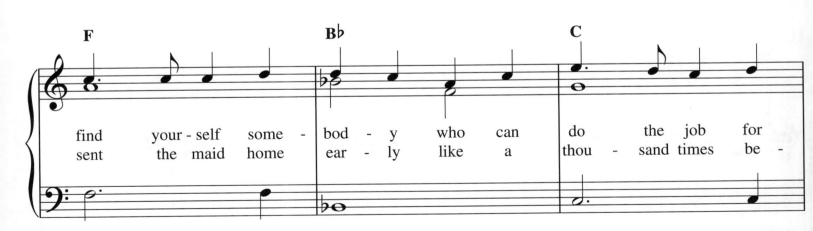

find your - self some -
sent the maid home

bod - y who can
ear - ly like a

do the job for
thou - sand times be -

free. _____
fore. _____

When you need a bit of
Like the cas - tle in his

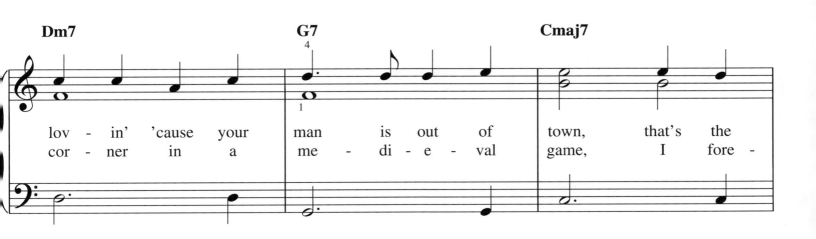

lov - in' 'cause your
cor - ner in a

man is out of
me - di - e - val

town, that's the
game, I fore -

time you get me
see ter - ri - ble

run - nin' and you
trou - ble and I

know I'll be a -
stay here just the

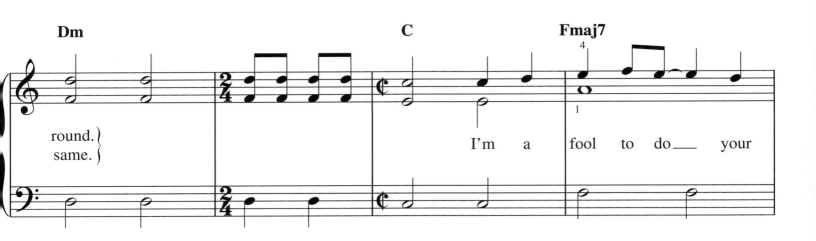

round.)
same.)

I'm a fool to do___ your

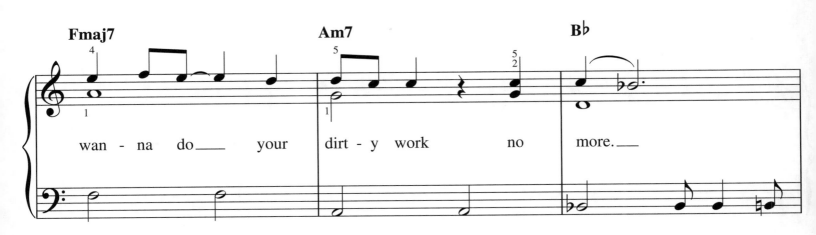

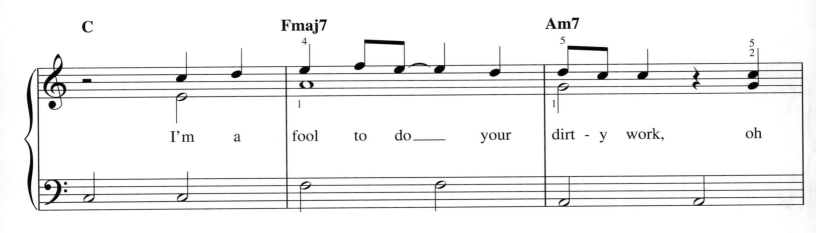

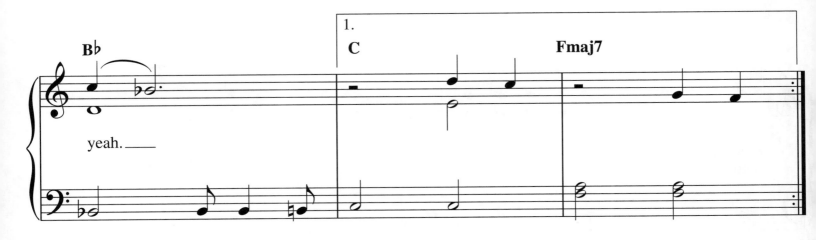

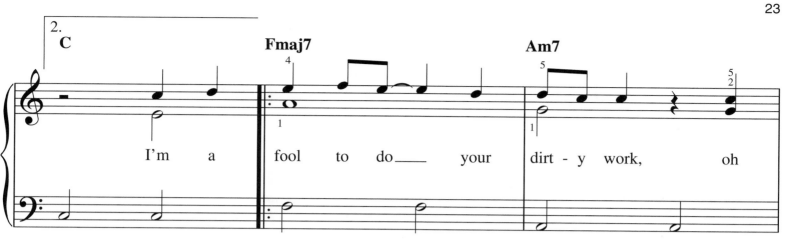

I'm a fool to do___ your dirt-y work, oh

yeah;___ I don't wan-na do___ your

Repeat and Fade

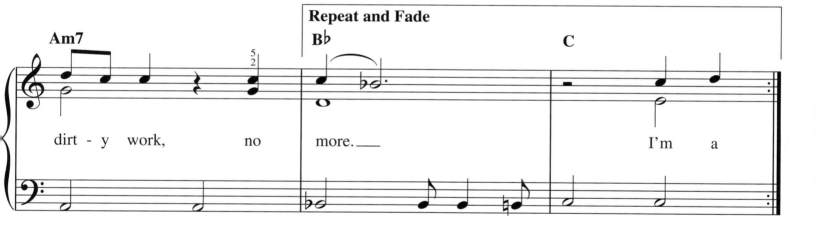

dirt-y work, no more.___ I'm a

Optional Ending

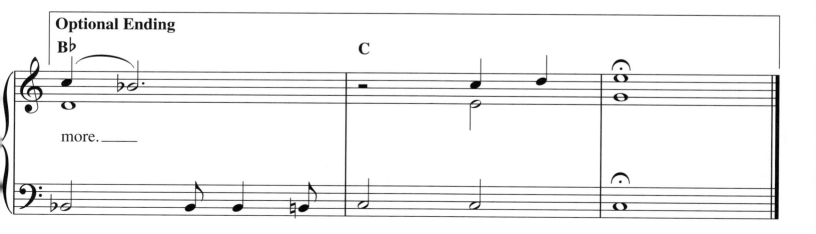

more.___

DO IT AGAIN

Words and Music by WALTER BECKER
and WALTER FAGEN

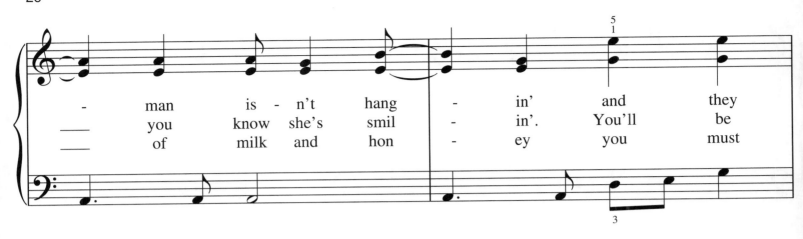

- man is - n't hang - in' and they
___ you know she's smil - in'. You'll be
___ of milk and hon - ey you must

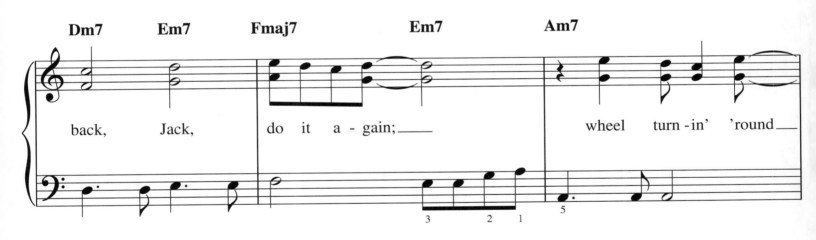

put you on the street. ___
on your knees to - mor - row. } Yeah, you go
put them on the ta - ble.

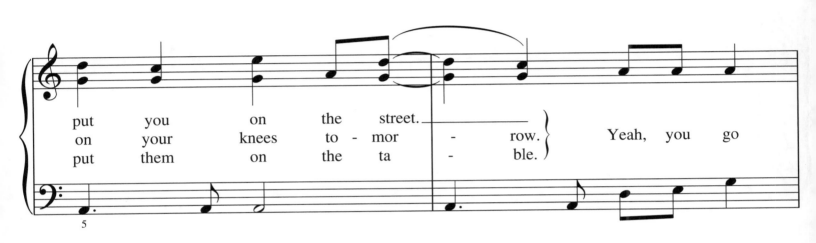

Dm7   Em7   Fmaj7   Em7   Am7

back, Jack, do it a - gain; ___ wheel turn - in' 'round ___

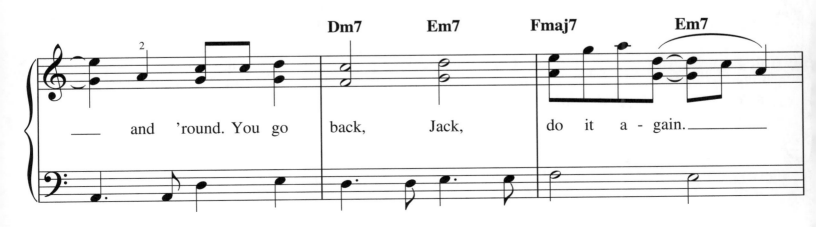

Dm7   Em7   Fmaj7   Em7

___ and 'round. You go back, Jack, do it a - gain. ___

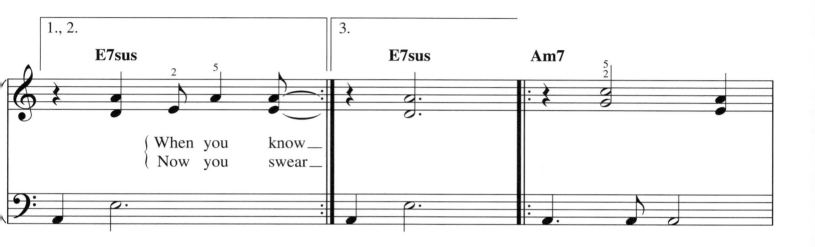

When you know___
Now you swear___

Repeat and Fade

Optional Ending

FM
from the film FM

Words and Music by WALTER BECKER
and DONALD FAGEN

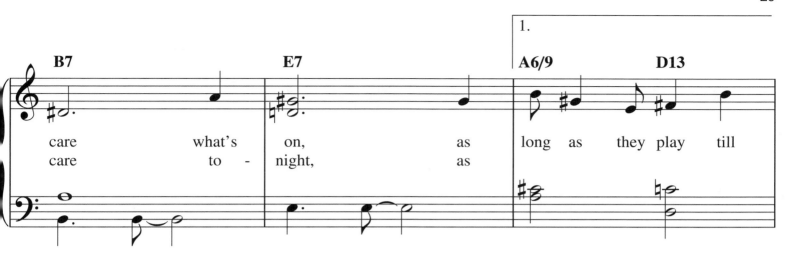

care   what's   on,   as   long   as   they play   till
care   to -   night,   as

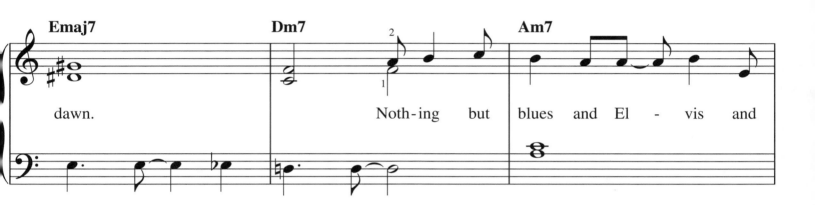

dawn.   Noth-ing   but   blues   and   El - vis   and

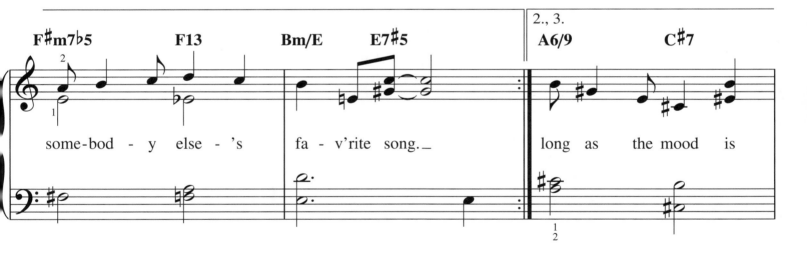

some-bod - y else - 's   fa - v'rite song._   long   as   the mood   is

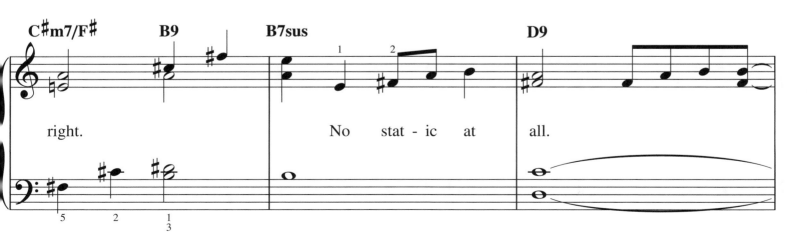

right.   No   stat - ic   at   all.

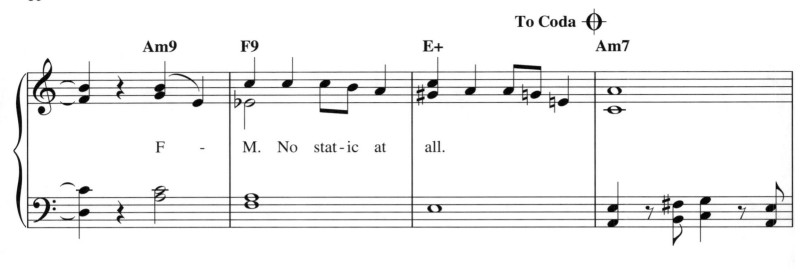

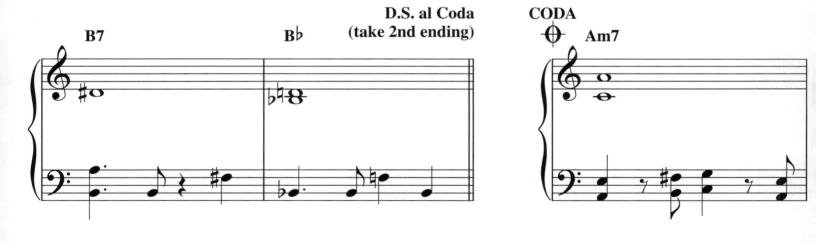

GAUCHO

Words and Music by WALTER BECKER,
DONALD FAGEN and KEITH JARRETT

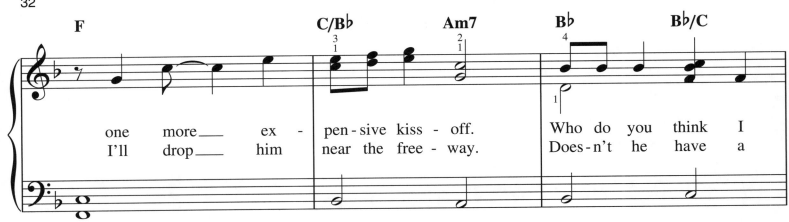

one more___ ex - pen - sive kiss - off.
I'll drop___ him near the free - way.

Who do you think I
Does - n't he have a

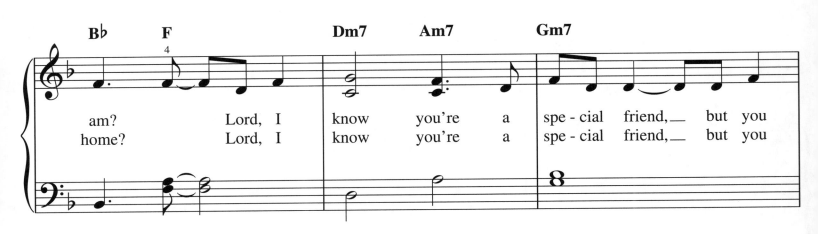

am? Lord, I know you're a spe - cial friend,___ but you
home? Lord, I know you're a spe - cial friend,___ but you

don't seem to un - der - stand.___ We got heav - y roll - ers, I
re - fuse to un - der - stand.___ You're a nas - ty school - boy with

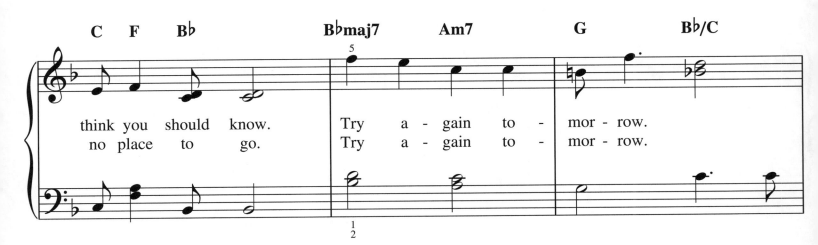

think you should know. Try a - gain to - mor - row.
no place to go. Try a - gain to - mor - row.

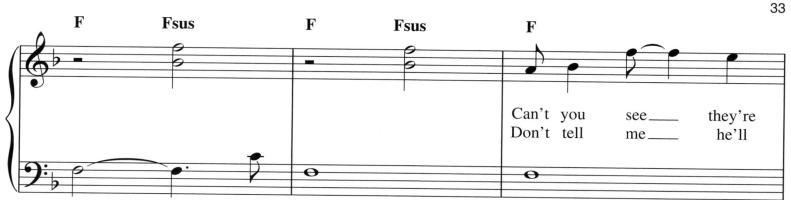

Can't you see____ they're
Don't tell me____ he'll

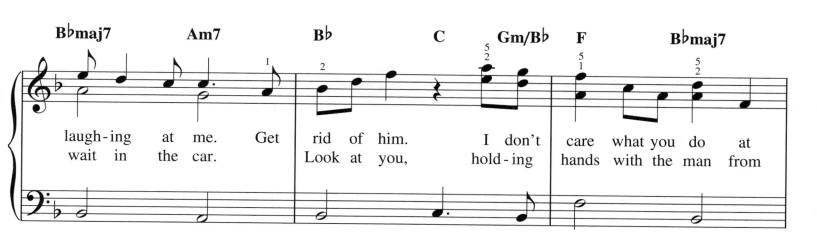

laugh-ing at me. Get
wait in the car. Look at you,

rid of him. I don't
hold-ing hands with the man from

home.
Ri - o.

Would you care to ex - plain?
Would you care to ex - plain?

Who is the gau - cho, a - mi - go?
Who is the gau - cho, a - mi - go?

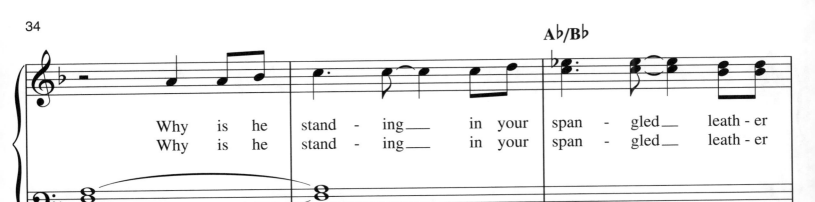

Why is he stand - ing___ in your span - gled___ leath - er
Why is he stand - ing___ in your span - gled___ leath - er

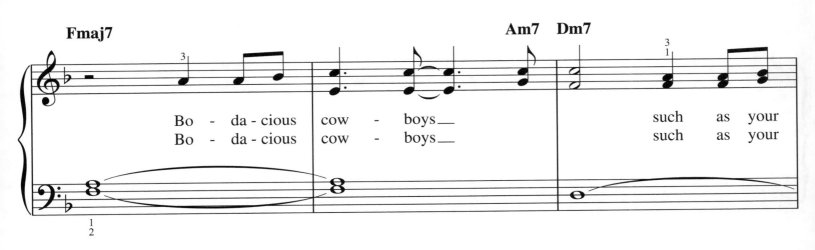

pon - cho_____ and your el - e - va - tor shoes?
pon - cho_____ with the studs that___ match your eyes?

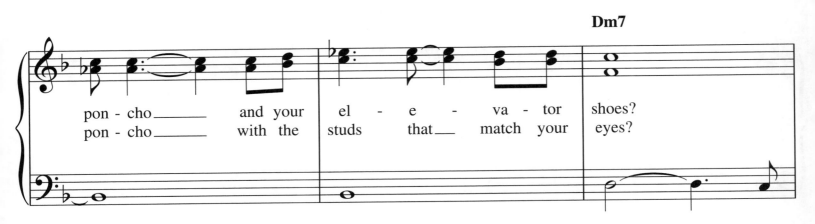

Bo - da - cious cow - boys___ such as your
Bo - da - cious cow - boys___ such as your

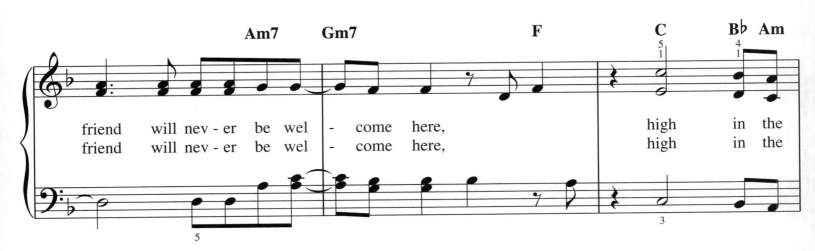

friend will nev - er be wel - come here, high in the
friend will nev - er be wel - come here, high in the

Cus - ter - dome.__
Cus - ter - dome.__

HEY NINETEEN

Words and Music by WALTER BECKER
and DONALD FAGEN

moved down___ to | Scars - dale. And where the | hell am I?
She thinks___ I'm | cra - zy, but I'm the just | grow - ing old.

Hey, Nine - teen, | no, we___ can't dance to -
Hey, Nine - teen, | no, we___ got noth - ing in

geth - er. } | No, we___ can't talk at all. | Please take me a -
com - mon. }

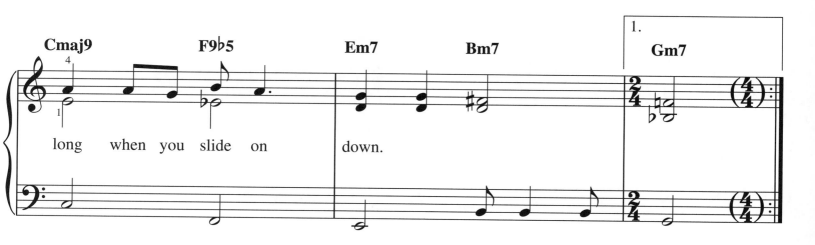

long when you slide on | down.

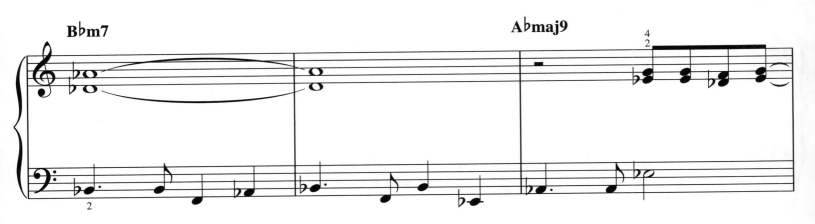

The Cuer - vo Gold,   the fine

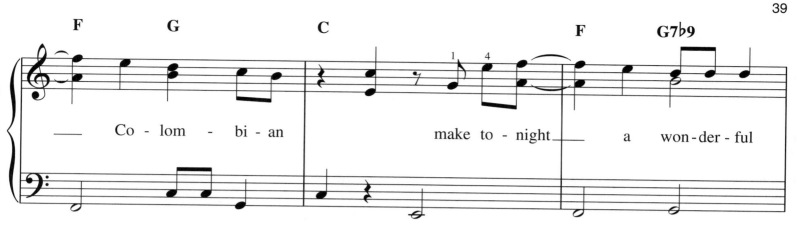

Co - lom - bi - an   make to - night ___ a won-der - ful

1.
thing.

2.
thing.

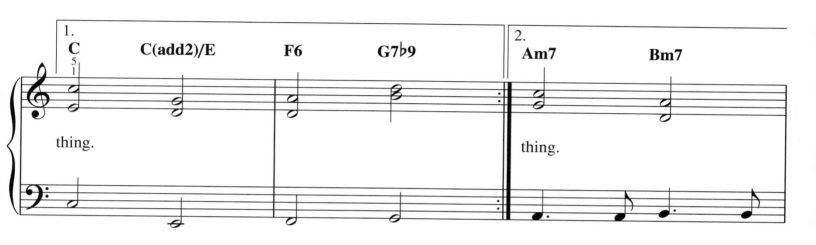

No,   we   can't   dance   to -

geth - er.   No,   we   can't   talk   at   all.

40

JOSIE

Words and Music by WALTER BECKER
and DONALD FAGEN

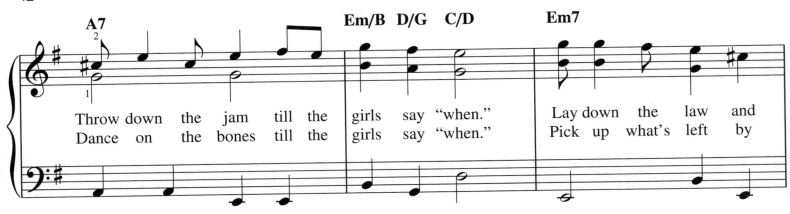

Throw down the jam till the girls say "when." Lay down the law and
Dance on the bones till the girls say "when." Pick up what's left by

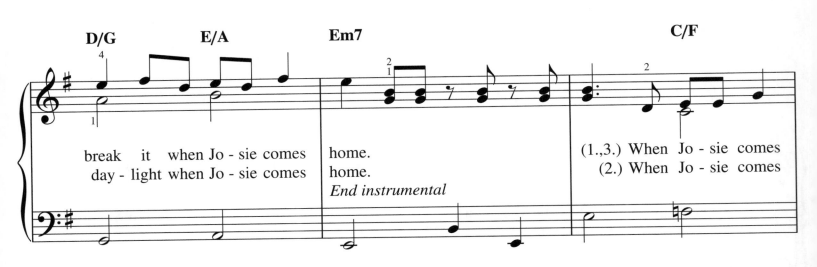

break it when Jo - sie comes home. (1.,3.) When Jo - sie comes
day - light when Jo - sie comes home. (2.) When Jo - sie comes
End instrumental

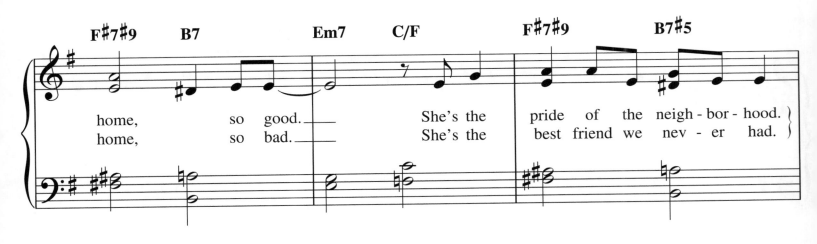

home, so good. She's the pride of the neigh - bor - hood.
home, so bad. She's the best friend we nev - er had.

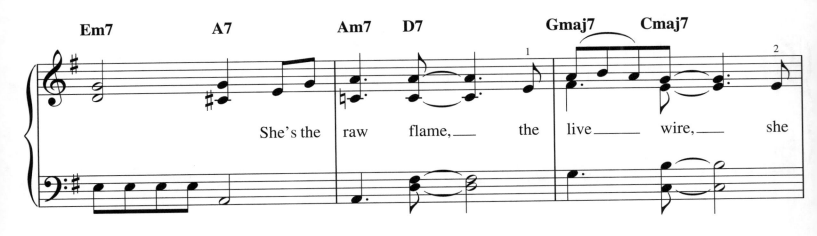

She's the raw flame, the live wire, she

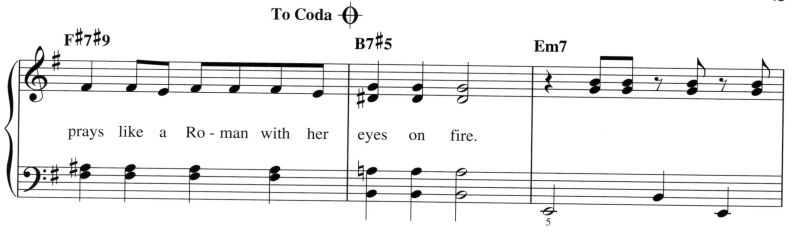

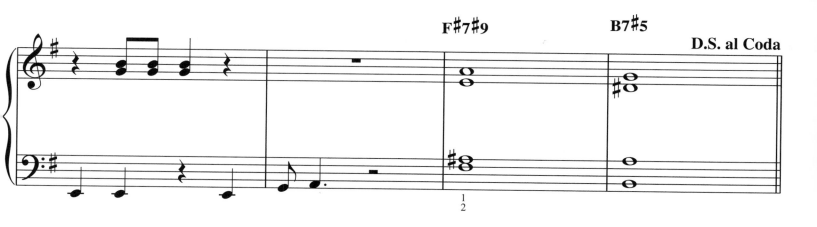

MY OLD SCHOOL

Words and Music by WALTER BECKER
and DONALD FAGEN

Moderately fast

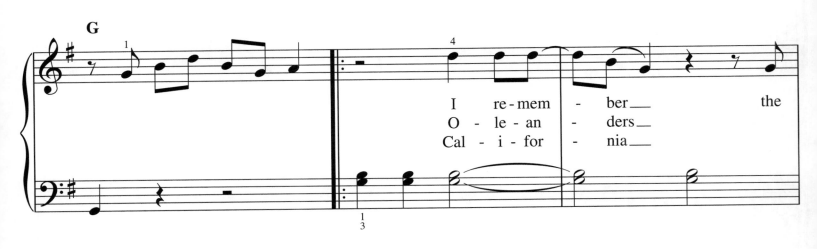

I re-mem - ber ___ the
O - le - an - ders ___
Cal - i - for - nia ___

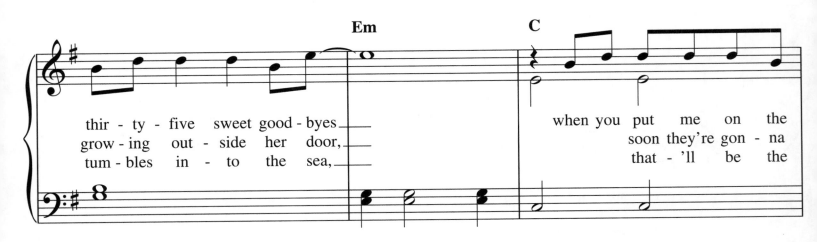

thir - ty - five sweet good - byes ___   when you put me on the
grow - ing out - side her door, ___   soon they're gon - na
tum - bles in - to the sea, ___   that - 'll be the

Wol - ver - ine ____ up in An - nan - dale.
be in bloom _ up in An - nan - dale.
day I go ____ back to An - nan - dale.

It was still Sep-tem - ber ___ when your dad-dy was quite sur-prised _
I can't stand ___ her ___ do - ing what she did be - fore, __
Tried to warn ___ you ___ a - bout Chi-no and Bud-dy Gee, __

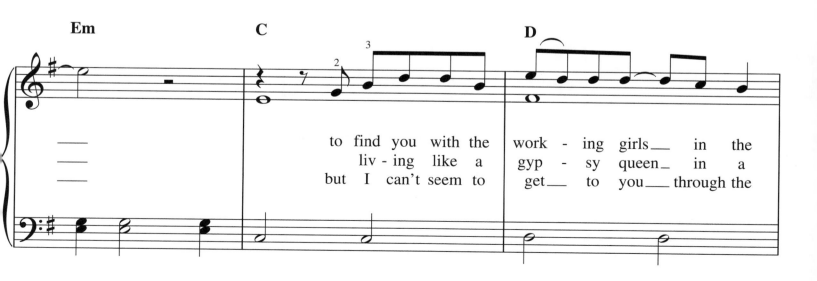

to find you with the work - ing girls ___ in the
liv - ing like a gyp - sy queen _ in a
but I can't seem to get __ to you __ through the

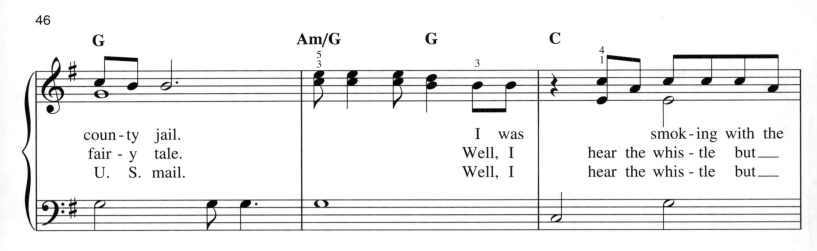

coun - ty jail.
fair - y tale.
U. S. mail.

I was smok - ing with the
Well, I hear the whis - tle but___
Well, I hear the whis - tle but___

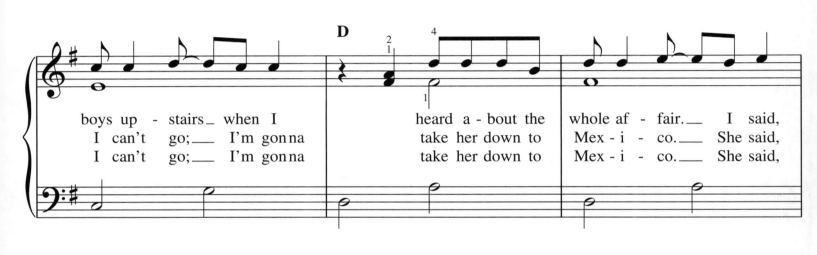

boys up - stairs___ when I
I can't go;___ I'm gonna
I can't go;___ I'm gonna

heard a - bout the whole af - fair.___ I said,
take her down to Mex - i - co.___ She said,
take her down to Mex - i - co.___ She said,

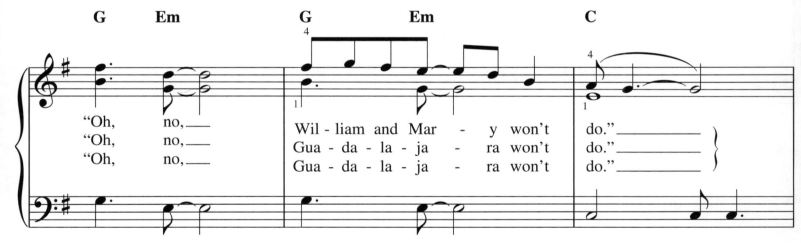

"Oh, no,___
"Oh, no,___
"Oh, no,___

Wil - liam and Mar - y won't do."___
Gua - da - la - ja - ra won't do."___
Gua - da - la - ja - ra won't do."___

Well, I did not think the girl___ could be so

PEG

Words and Music by WALTER BECKER
and DONALD FAGEN

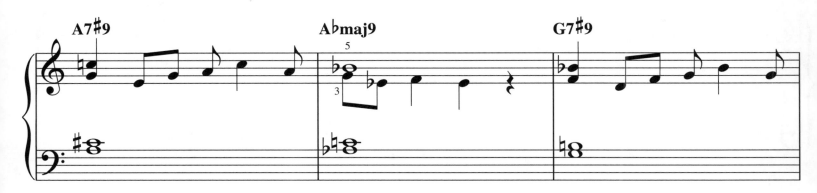

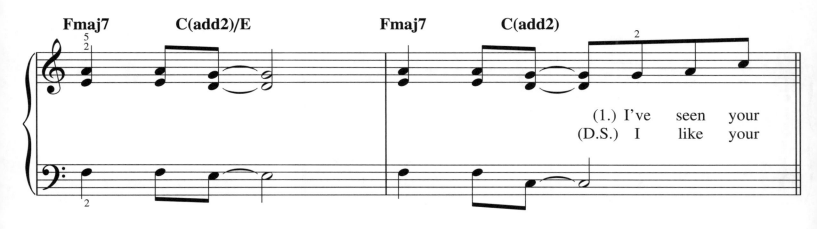

(1.) I've seen your
(D.S.) I like your

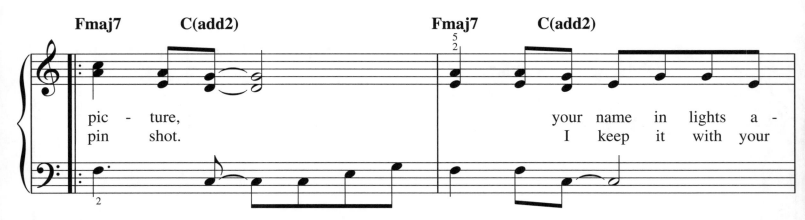

pic - ture,
pin shot.

your name in lights a -
I keep it with your

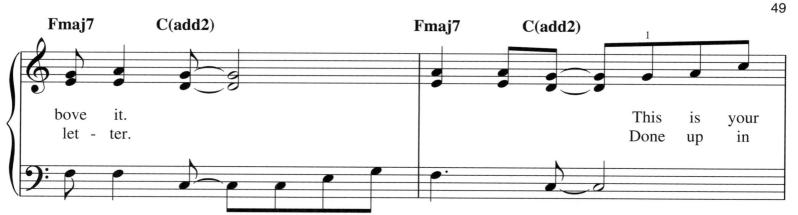

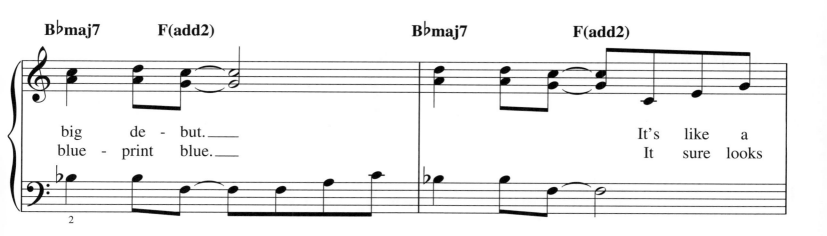

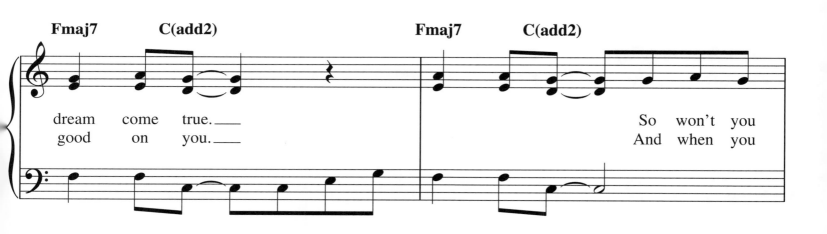

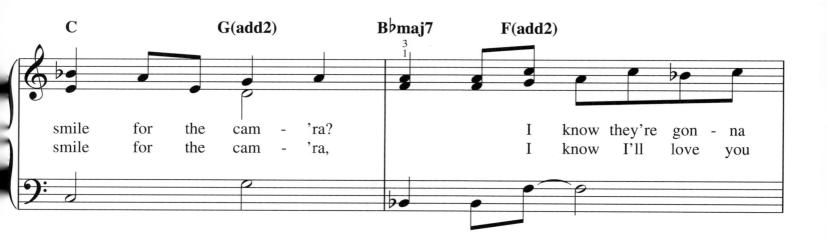

love it. Peg. I like your bet-ter.

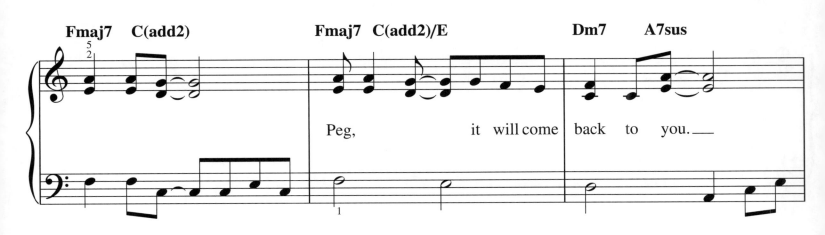

Peg, it will come back to you.___

Peg, it will come back to you.___ Then___ the shut-ter

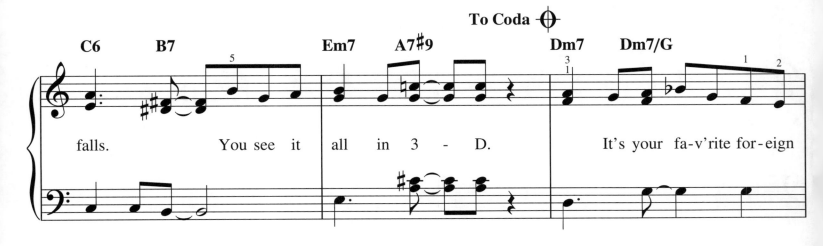

falls. You see it all in 3 - D. It's your fa-v'rite for-eign

REELING IN THE YEARS

Words and Music by WALTER BECKER
and DONALD FAGEN

Your ev - er - last - in' sum - mer, you can
tell - in' me you're a gen - ius since
spent a lot of mon - ey and I

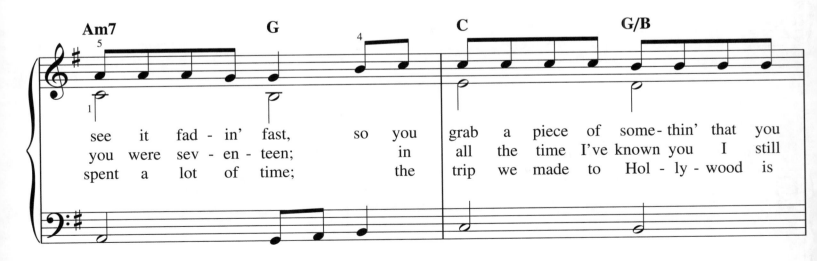

see it fad - in' fast, so you
you were sev - en - teen; in
spent a lot of time; the

grab a piece of some - thin' that you
all the time I've known you I still
trip we made to Hol - ly - wood is

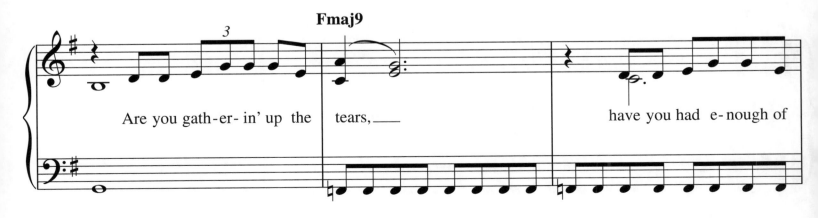

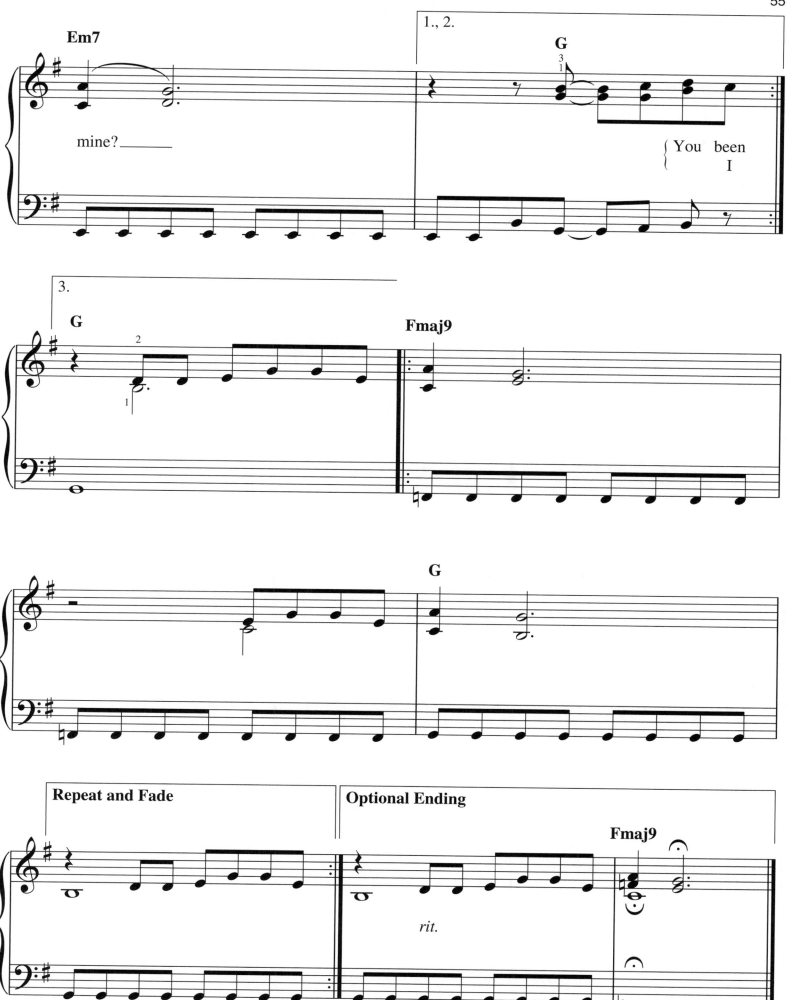

RIKKI DON'T LOSE THAT NUMBER

Words and Music by WALTER BECKER
and DONALD FAGEN

I guess you kind of scared your-self, you turn ___ and run. ___
We could stay in - side and play games, I ___ don't know. _

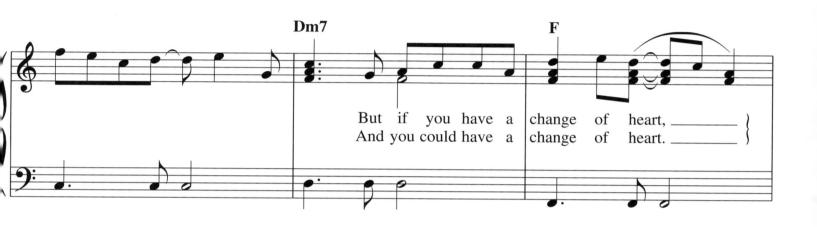

But if you have a change of heart, _____ }
And you could have a change of heart. _____ }

Rik-ki, don't lose that num - ber; you don't wan-na

call no-bod - y else. Send it off in a

let - ter   to your -   self.

Rik - ki, don't   lose   that num -   ber; _____   it's the   on - ly   one you   own. _

_   You might   use it   if   you   feel   bet - ter

To Coda ⊕

when you get   home.

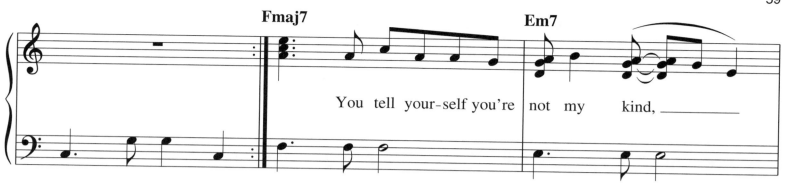

Fmaj7

Em7

You tell your-self you're not my kind, _____

Fmaj7

Am7

Dm7

but you don't e - ven know your mind. _____ And you could have a

F

N.C.

D.S. al Coda

change of heart. _____

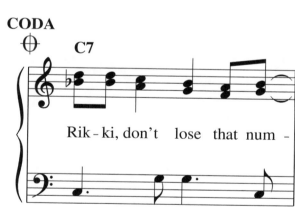

CODA

C7

Rik - ki, don't lose that num -

- ber.

Rik - ki, don't lose that num - ber. _____

TIME OUT OF MIND

Words and Music by WALTER BECKER
and DONALD FAGEN

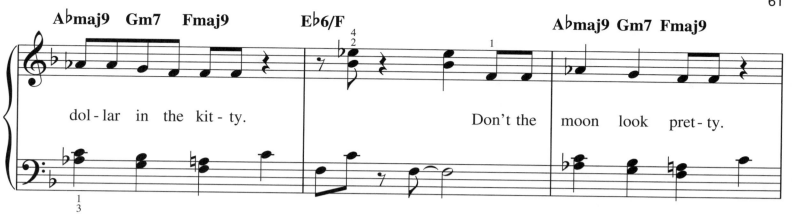

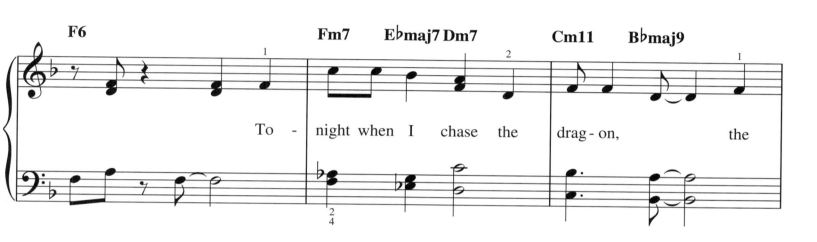

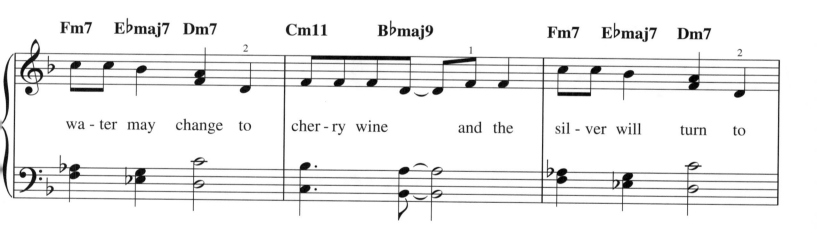

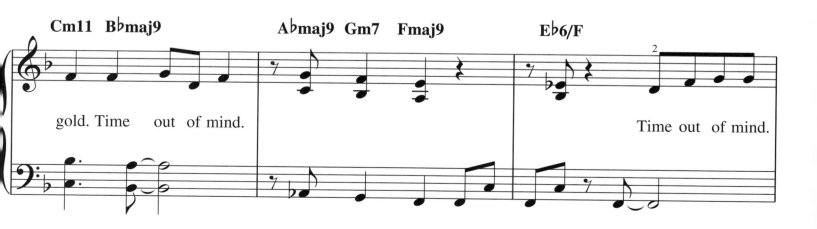

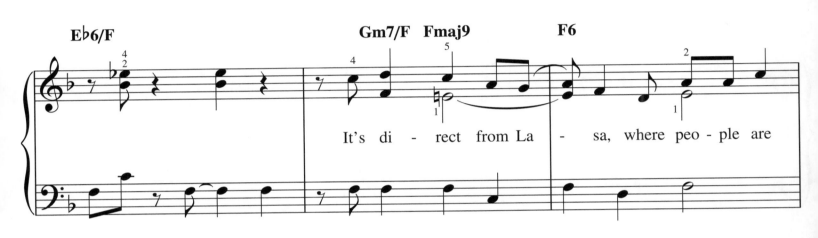

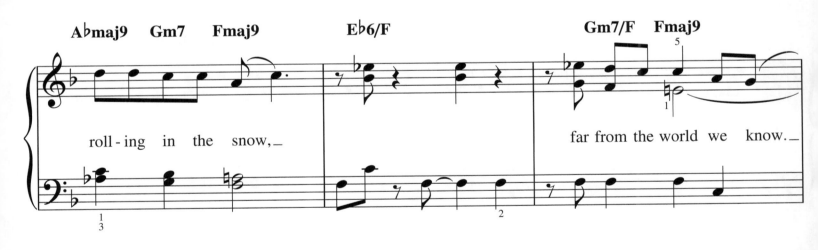

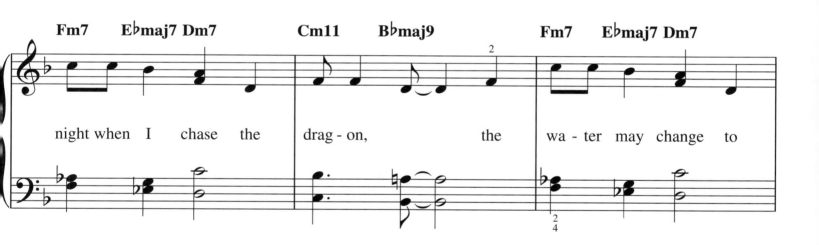

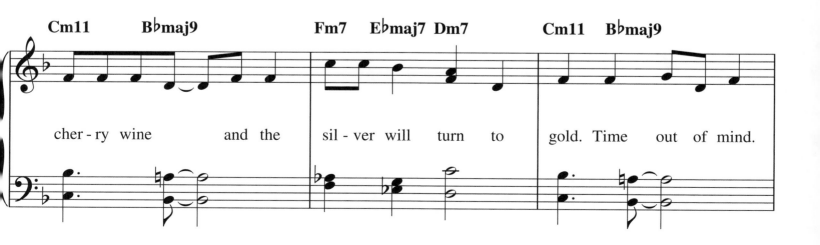